Mortimer's Fun with Words

Rhyming Words

Karen Bryant-Mole

Gareth Stevens Publishing
A WORLD ALMANAC EDUCATION GROUP COMPANY

Mortimer's Fun with Words

For a free color catalog describing Gareth Stevens' list of high-quality books and multimedia programs, call 1-800-542-2595 (USA) or 1-800-461-9120 (Canada). Gareth Stevens Publishing's Fax: (414) 332-3567.

Library of Congress Cataloging-in-Publication Data available upon request from publisher. Fax: (414) 332-3567 for the attention of the Publishing Records Department.

ISBN 0-8368-2751-1

This North American edition first published in 2000 by
Gareth Stevens Publishing
A World Almanac Education Group Company
330 West Olive Street, Suite 100
Milwaukee, WI 53212 USA

This edition © 2000 by Gareth Stevens, Inc. Original © BryantMole Books, 1999. First published in 1999 by Evans Brothers Limited, 2A Portman Mansions, Chiltern Street, London W1M 1LE, United Kingdom. Additional end matter © 2000 by Gareth Stevens, Inc.

Created by Karen Bryant-Mole
Photographs by Zul Mukhida
Designed by Jean Wheeler
Teddy bear by Merrythought Ltd.

Printed in the United States of America

1 2 3 4 5 6 7 8 9 04 03 02 01 00

contents

...ug

Mortimer is giving the bug a hug.

The words **bug** and **hug** rhyme.

Two of these things rhyme
with **bug** and **hug**.

Can you name them?

Mortimer is going to chat with a rat.

The words **chat** and **rat** rhyme.

One of these things rhymes
with **chat** and **rat**.

Can you find it?

...ig and ...an

Mortimer is wearing a big green wig!

The words **big** and **wig** rhyme.

Can you find something that
rhymes with **big** and **wig**?

Now find two things that
rhyme with **man**.

...og and ...ag

Mortimer is going to jog with a dog.

The words **jog** and **dog** rhyme.

Can you find something
that rhymes with **jog**
and **dog**?

Now find two things that
rhyme with **wag**.

...ock and ...ing

Mortimer's clock goes tick, tock.

The words **clock** and **tock** rhyme.

Can you find something that rhymes with **clock** and **tock**?

Now find two things that rhyme with **wing**.

...oon and ...ee

Mortimer wants to go to the moon soon.

The words **moon** and **soon** rhyme.

Can you find something that rhymes with **moon** and **soon**?

Now find two things that rhyme with **knee**.

...ake and ...ane

Mortimer knows how to bake a cake.

The words **bake** and **cake** rhyme.

Can you find something that rhymes with **bake** and **cake**?

Now find two things that rhyme with **mane**.

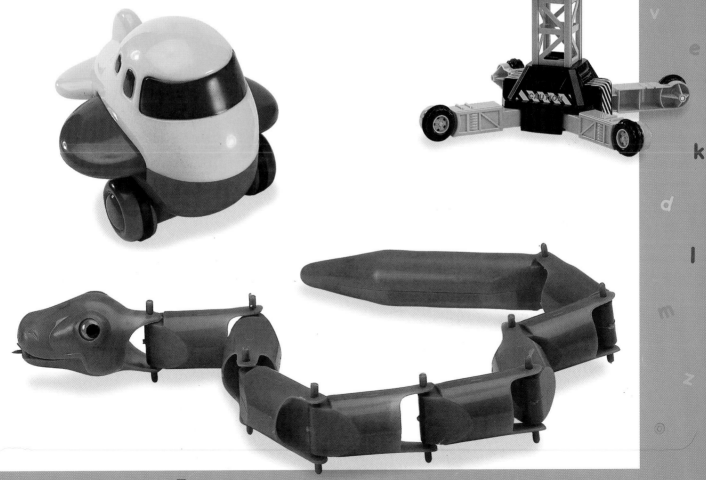

...oat and ...own

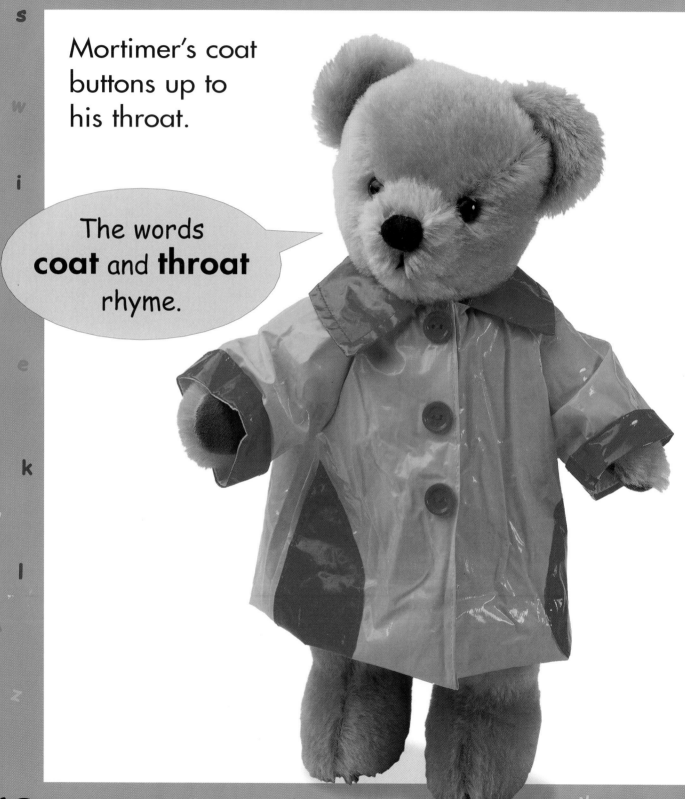

Mortimer's coat buttons up to his throat.

The words **coat** and **throat** rhyme.

18

Can you find something that rhymes with **coat** and **throat**?

Now find another pair of rhyming words.

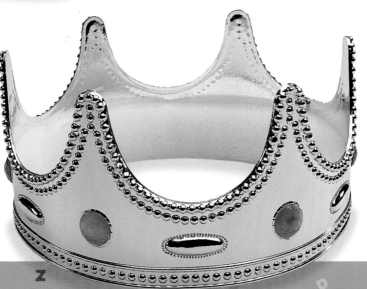

Mortimer sees another bear over there.

The words **bear** and **there** rhyme.

Can you find something that rhymes with **bear** and **there** and ends with the letters ...**air**?

Now find another pair of words that rhymes with **tail** but ends in different letters.

find the pairs

Can you find three pairs of rhyming words?

22

glossary/index

bake — to cook something in an oven 16, 17

bug — an insect or other small, creepy-crawly creature 4, 5

chat — to talk to someone in a friendly way 6, 7

clock — a device that shows what time it is 12, 13

jog — to run at a slow and even speed 10, 11

mane — thick, long hair such as that around a lion's face or along a horse's neck 17

pair — a set of two things 19, 21, 22

rat — a kind of rodent that looks like a mouse, but is bigger and has a longer tail 6, 7

soon — happening in a short period of time; before long 14, 15

wag — to move or swing back and forth or up and down, like the way a dog moves its tail 11

wig — a covering for the head that is made of real or artificial hair 8, 9

videos

Barney Rhymes with Mother Goose. (Lyons Group)

Barney's Rhyme Time Rhythm. (Lyrick Studios)

Richard Scarry's Best Learning Songs Video Ever! (Sony Wonder)